Heart And Soul

CONTENTS

Acknowledgements

I wish to thank all those who inspired me in the writing of
<u>**Heart and Soul: A Poetic Journey Since 9/11**</u>:

My dear God who gave me a heart and soul with which to write
and my family for their constant support and encouragement:
My **Mom** and **Dad** who told me to write this book for years and years
My son **Chris,** whose faith in me never dies
Marisa, Chris's fiancé
Kari Okie, my puppy and my best friend
My sisters **Theresa** and **Jacqueline**
My "brothers" **Michael J.** and **Anthony**
My nephews **Anthony J.** and **Daniel**
And **Lauren** (Anthony J.'s girlfriend)

My friends **Vivian, Marsha-Ann, Joe G., Joe L., Barbara L., Monica E., Ron. E., Linda S., Bella, Ann Marie Renzi,** my cover designer and friend
Cynthia Hanratty, my editor and friend
Cathy Sullivan, my lawyer and friend for her dedication and loyalty
Edward Khusid, who told me to "Write it all down"
Michael Lapidus, for insuring my sanity and for his encouragement

And in loving memory of Jack E Blu
This Book Got Written Because of You

The Eulogy of John T. (Jack) Andreacchio

"Captain Jack"

Written by Chris Lentini

"Captain Jack"

Eulogy for Jack Andreacchio
Written by Christopher J. Lentini on 10/5/01
Read by Christopher at Jack's Funeral on 10/6/01 at
St. Simon & Jude R.C. Church

The first time I heard his voice on the phone I knew he was trying to get on my good side and he quickly tried to bribe me with some Mets tickets. "Hey Chris, I have some tickets to the Mets/Expos game, would you be interested in going?" he asked. As I was contemplating this obvious attempt to butter up the son of his new girlfriend, at first I was cautious. "Well, I don't know," and before I could get another word out he said, "Man, I hate it when someone can't make up their mind!" Little did I know how big of a Yankees fan he was, and how many battles we would end up having over our favorite baseball teams, but from that point on, I knew I was dealing with a character and a half.

Jack, as we all know, was more than just a character. He was someone who always "shot from the hip," and told it like it was, in true cowboy style. When I left too much water on the bathroom sink, enough to wet his clothes when he leaned against it... I heard about it. When I put on enough powder to blanket most of our bathroom and choke just about anyone who came in after me... I heard about it. And when we first got America Online, and Jack and I shared the bill and it totaled more than his favorite pair of cowboy boots... I heard about it. But Jack let me know about it in a way that a friend would tell another friend. He would say just enough to let you know he didn't like it, but he would put up with it. For some reason now I find myself cleaning off the bathroom sink, not using as much powder, and well let's just say I am thankful that the America Online bill is just one easy payment of $24.00 a month.

Some of you may have known Jack to be an amateur and I do mean amateur comedian. I think I heard him say this one about a thousand times "Chris, you know why I don't like basketball? (No, why Jack?) 'Cause I hate to see grown men dribble." That would be followed by his trademark laugh. I always thought that joke was pretty bad all those times I heard it. But you know what? Now, I find myself thinking that's the funniest joke I ever heard.

Jack was also known for being a party animal. Whether it was drinking with kids half his age on our trip to Ocean City, Maryland, dancing the Boot Scootin' Boogie with my mom on a trip to Tennessee, singing his favorite Garth Brooks hit "Friends in Low Places" on the karaoke machine or doing his memorable "dip and rip my pants" move at my high school graduation party, Jack always knew how to have a good time. There were many more times that Jack was the life of the party, just too many to talk about. He lived his life on his terms and that meant living life to the fullest, and that's something we can all learn from him.

Jack has been to more places, met more people, and done more things in his life than some people will ever do in a hundred lifetimes. I can honestly say he has influenced every life he touched in one way or another. I know he influenced me personally in many ways. From a simple "Good morning, Chris" as he would start making coffee at around 5:30 am and I would be finishing up a report for school, to helping me with learning to drive in many scary trips around the complex in Pennsylvania, to teaching me how to tie a tie, pushing me to explore talents that he felt I had, to just being a friend when I needed one, Jack was always there for me. I sometimes, as usually is the case with those who are close to us, took him for granted and for that I am sorry. But, if I know Jack like I do, I'm sure he would say "Ah, forget about it Chris."

Jack also taught us to put others ahead of ourselves and he showed many examples of this by giving and raising money for charities, showing groups of high school kids from my Mom's school the inner workings of an international bank and creating a "Fuji Bank Career Day," giving up his free time to help organize the Fuji Bank Christmas Party, and also becoming a leader of Fuji's emergency evacuation committee, a job that he took very seriously.

None of us will ever know what actually happened inside World Trade Center Two on September 11th, but you can rest assured that Jack Andreacchio acted heroically and selflessly and assisted many people to safety. He was not only a hero on that day, but everyday. His main goal in life was to be happy and to lift the spirits of as many people as he could. His spirit will always remain with each one of us and he will help us to heal in our time of need. He will have more influence on our lives now than ever before.

I tried to think of a famous quote that was suitable for Jack, and I came up with something that is a combination of a quote that was used when Ted Kennedy eulogized his brother Bobby and some of my own thoughts. "Jack saw it broke and tried to fix it, he saw a wrong and tried to right it, he saw it hurt and tried to help it."

Jack sees us all hurting right now and although he knows it will take some time, he would want us to continue to live our lives to the fullest as he taught us so many times before.

Poems written by loved ones before I could write...

"WTC Prayer for All" by Marsha-Ann DeFatta

"Jack E Blu" by Jacqueline Lombardi

Marsha-Ann's WTC Prayer to All

Written By Marsha-Ann DeFatta
9/11/01

Two mountains crumbled by the sea
Oh Lord
Please give us strength to overcome our tragedy
Our beloved Jack* walks with you
And all who were met with open arms
Maybe in time
Can we heal our pain?
For good will overcome all
Please bless our new angels and heroes
And give us peace and love to go forward

* Any name can be placed here

Jack E Blu

By Jacqueline Lombardi
Dedicated to Jack Andreacchio
9/23/01

Jack E Blu
Where are you?
We miss you so
Why did you go?

You had to help
That was your style
When danger struck
You took awhile

You didn't leave
You didn't run
They all came first
Except for one

You needed help
It came too late
A hero by far
A man too great

We all love you
We're all so proud
We'll never forget
We solemnly vow

7/26/03

This is a book about pain, loss and shock. It is a journey through grief, as I experienced it, in my heart and soul. It is written in the only form that I am comfortable with-poems. I hope that you will find some comfort through my emotional journey.

Francine Skye Morales Lentini

The Preface

By Francine Skye Lentini
7/26/03

Why was this book written?
When did it begin?
The poems are almost simple
They're just thoughts that came from within

It wasn't written for intellects
It wasn't written for fame
It was written to express my feelings
And to say thank you to all of "them"

Those heroes without any recognition
Who put their own lives on the line
To help many others make it through
And by risking all didn't survive

This book was also written for the families
And the loved ones left behind
Who are still trying to overcome the shock
And trying to survive these times

This book was also written
To tell the story of me and Jack E Blu
To show my journey through grief since Jack's loss
And the pain and disbelief I went through

I asked many "experts" to help me
To understand the horrific truth
But I found nothing that I could really relate to
And my emotions remained confused

I was told to write down my feelings
On Fathers Day, 2002, my written journey began
The words that were confined in my heart and soul
Found their way to the pen in my hand

I hope that my poems could help others
Who have a broken heart, to heal
Then I'd feel as if I've accomplished my purpose
To satisfy a need that's so real

In Memory of My Beloved Hero
Jack E Blu Andreacchio

And To All The Heroes of 9/11
The Sung
and The Unsung

MY POEMS

Missing Blu

By Francine Skye Lentini
6/16/02

You are always on my mind
You are always in my heart
My arms still reach to touch you
You're not there; I'm torn apart

Your memory lives within me
I miss you more each day
When I close my eyes each night
It's to dream of you I pray

My soul is always crying
It's missing an important part
It's mate is now in Heaven
Where it's living with my heart

And every day I talk to you
I wish an angel for your guide
You will find your peace in Heaven
God will keep you by his side

From here you did depart
To God's Eternal Resting Place
He'll welcome you into His arms
You're a hero, now a saint

As I lie in bed without you
And try to mend this broken heart
I ask Our Lord to help me
And to tell me how to start

So look down on me from heaven
My loving angel from above
And pray for me, your "Lil' Darlin' "
To find some healing, peace and love

Your Ever-Lovin' Cowgirl, Skye

Jack E Blu My Lovin' Cowboy

By Francine Skye Lentini
6/16/02

Jack E Blu, my lovin' cowboy
Where did you go? What did you do?
You gave your life for others
Now the Lord is holding you

Look down on me from heaven
Please always be by my side
Lead me in the right direction
Ask God to be my guide

Help me find peace and rest here
Truth and Respect are what I seek
A consolation for my grieving
Please ask the Lord for me

Now we know you're His angel
Protect me as I go
Trying to live life without you
Is the hardest road I know

And just when I start thinking
I might make it through the day
My heart starts re-breaking
And my tears fall away

I know you're always with me
If I could hold you one more time
I'd feel alive inside me
Your soul entwined with mine

I'll love you always and forever
It just gets harder every day
How to live life without you
For an answer, I'll always pray

Did He Know He Was My Hero

By Francine Skye Lentini
6/16/02

(Words were running 'round my head
"Write for Blu is what they said"
I asked, "How should I begin it? Where should I start?
He was the love of my life. He was the man of my
heart)

We liked the same places
We liked the same things
I was his princess
He was my king

He always brought me flowers
He said I deserved the best
He said he loved me for my heart
He didn't care about the rest

He said he'd love me if I were thin
He said he'd love me if I were fat
He said he loved me because of me
And I loved him more for that

I loved the way he laughed
I loved that he could cry
When watching sad old movies
Or when feeling sad inside

He was a loving, gentle, man
He loved his cowgirl Skye
He loved his pal and buddy
He taught Chris to tie his tie

He loved our country dancing
"Boot Scootin' Boogie" is how we met
All the time we spent together
Was the time we spent the best

He loved living in the country
He called Blu Skye Ranch our home
He loved our summer vacations
When to Nashville we would roam

He loved his flag; he loved his country
He loved his darlin' wife
He loved his job; he loved his friends
And for them he gave his life

He will always be my hero
My Blu I will always love
But did he know he was my hero
Before he went to God above?

He'll always be a patriot
For all the world to see
I pray I'll always be his "Skyegirl"
Who he'll love eternally

Souls Entwined Forever

By Francine Skye Lentini
6/16/02

I wanted to pray for you tonight
I took my prayer book to bed
My eyes began to fill with tears
So I cried all night instead

But when I wake tomorrow morning
I'll try to start another day
Then I'll see the day grow harder
Without your loving ways

I was always your "Lil' Darlin'"
My cowboy "Blu" you'll always be
Our "Blu Skye Ranch" is still waiting
A return from you and me

Now how am I supposed to go there?
Without Jack E Blu by my side
How can I look around there?
Knowing Blu has left his Skye

Cowboy Blu, you died a hero
You went to heaven, leaving me
But I just can't stop this crying
'Cause "over you," I'll never be

I hope that in the future
As we have in the past
We can entwine our souls forever
And our love will everlast

Where Are You Jack E Blu?

By Francine Skye Lentini
6/16/02

I looked for you on TV
I looked for you outside
I awaited your arrival
Chris and Kari by my side

We stayed by the phone each night
We looked outside at 6 PM
We didn't miss a newscast
We were comforted by our friends

Kari Okie barked nightly
At the time you should've been home
Chris and crew looked in the city
To see where you had roamed

Each day became a nightmare
Each night became surreal
No longer eating; no longer sleeping
Not understanding if this was real

Days turned into weeks
Then after three you were found
In scattered bits and pieces
Among the rubble on the ground

The day I saw them crumble
The day the Towers fell
From my school's locker-room window
I saw the smoke rise from hell

I ran out of school screaming
My guardian angel by my side
I drove home in shocked silence
Turned on the TV, then I cried

When you were finally found
I had no rights and no respect
I was looked upon as no one
I stood by you nonetheless

I still look to you for answers
I still look to you to say,
"You are still my L'il Darlin' "
"And I love you more each day"

I miss your loving kisses
I miss your tender touch
I miss the words you always said
That touched my heart so much

I miss the way you loved me
I miss you by my side
I miss our life together
I miss you calling me "Skye"

It gets harder living without you
It gets harder every day
"How Can I Live Without You?"
Trisha sang it the best way

I will still try to find you
In the air I breathe each day
In the stars that shine above me
In the woods down by the bay

In the lake or in the ocean
Or are you at Heaven's door
Or do I look inside my heart
Where I'll love you evermore

9/11/01 Thank Yous

Written by Francine Skye Lentini
6/16/02

Now, whom should I be thanking
Since the towers had to fall
And killed my loving husband
Who stayed behind to help them all?

First I thank Our Father
God was kind to spare my son
I couldn't bear to lose them both
But He needed to take one

I thank my son for his support
When I couldn't even stand
He took my hand and led me
Showing all that he's a man

I am always thankful to my parents
For remaining by my side
Offering love and consolation
Their advice is always wise

And thanks dear friends and loved ones
For supporting Chris and I
When you went to the memorial
To get Jack's urn with pride

Thank you dear Marisa
For your support we hold so dear
And to my "best friend," Kari Okie
My puppy who's always near

So to all who helped to comfort us
And who shared their love each day
I pray our Lord will bless you
In His divine and caring way

Unconditional

By Francine Skye Lentini
6/18/02

Unconditional, That's how you loved
That's why you were sent to heaven above

Unconditional, That's how you gave
For charity, for love, to help, to save

Unconditional, That's how you lived
Never holding back; giving all you had to give

Unconditional, That's how you served
To family, friends and colleagues; no reserve

Unconditional Love, is what God wants from us all
You knew how to give it, and you answered His call

Unconditionally, you loved God and the USA
And for God and country you died that day

Unconditional love is what I thought I knew
Now I truly understand it now because of Jack E Blu

Still Missing You

By Francine Skye
7/14/02

I reached out to touch you but you weren't there
I reached over to kiss you but my lips remained bare
I tried to cuddle with you but you weren't in our bed
A teddy bear was nearby so I hugged it instead

I reached out to call you, but no answer came
Only silence returned when I called out your name
I kept trying to phone you; only stillness rang through
Now whatever I'm doing, I'm still missing you

It's about the way you called me when you came home
It's about the way you hugged me when we were alone
It's about the way we snuggled when we went to bed
It's about the way you phoned me and the words that
        you said

Where are your footsteps when you close the door?
Why don't I hear "Honey I'm home," anymore?
I will never get used to living my life this way
I'm still missing you with each passing day

Waking Up Is Hard To Do

By Francine Skye Lentini
7/15/02

Today when I woke up
I didn't want to get out of bed
It just seemed too hard
To start the day ahead

I have a loving family
And many caring friends
They stand by to carry me
When I feel I've reached my end

God gave me my parents
And my son; a wonderful man
Each helps me to go on
The best way that they can

They help to ease my sorrow
They help to ease my pain
They all encourage me to go on
And to live my life again

But this morning when I woke up
I felt so sad and blue
I miss the life we shared
And the things we used to do

I miss our love, our thoughts, our plans, our prayers
Everyone tells me to make a new start
But how can I begin to live
With such a heavy heart?

I'm really trying hard
To make it through every day
Does time make it easier?
That's what people say

So then I ask them to tell me
Why, after ten months, do I still feel?
Like you should be here with me
And that none of this is real

Why is it that even after I saw
The Twin Towers crashing down
Do I still look to talk to you
And still think that you're around

My mind says you've gone
To a much better place
But my heart says you're still here
And I expect to see your face

I know I have to heal
And get on with my life
I just don't know how to do it
Without being your wife

I keep coming back
To the inevitable truth
I can't bear to face the change
Of living without you

You made my life bearable
You made me complete
Now I'm having trouble
Standing on my own two feet

Lately I've been told by priests
That you could pray for me
So if you could, would you ask God
To send the comfort that I need?

And if it's at all possible
And you could find the time
Could you whisper in my ear
And tell me everything will be fine?

And lastly, could you help me
From your perch so high above
And ask the Lord to show me
How to live without your love

Give Thanks To God?

By Francine Skye Lentini
7/17/02

Why should I be thankful?
Because I'm alive and here
I think, "Life stinks," "That's right!"
Just look anywhere
"Others" have the riches
The mansions, and the jewels
They have no worries
No problems
No hunger and
No bills

Everywhere I look I see
More hate
More prejudice
More wars
Violence
Hunger
Evil
Strife
Too many problems to ignore

I go to work, to toil, to sweat every day
Never any appreciation
Never enough pay
Polluted air
Polluted soil

Polluted water
Polluted minds
So tell me why should I be thankful
For what has become of mankind?

But if I look on the other side
Then maybe I will know
That God gave each of us an answer
Through the love that He has shown
He gave me a heart and a soul
And taught me of evil to beware
He helps me through all life's valleys
With just a simple prayer
No problem is too great with the help of my Lord
No matter what it might be
"If you ask, it will be given"
That is our destiny

I find I can be grateful
For my family, and my friends
And I should thank God for each blessing
That He so generously sends

My Crazy Advocate

By Francine Skye Lentini
7/17/02

We had a strange beginning
And like many friendships go
A need of mine, a concern of yours
We met ten months ago

You said you were a lawyer
Working "pro bono" for the Bar
I was impressed when we spoke
I knew you would go far

When I told you that my lawyers
Were picked by the UFT
You said, very quickly,
"Go with them instead of me"

I had an answer for you
I knew right from the start
I didn't want to go to them
If then we'd have to part

You said you could be my "Advocate,"
And you could still work with me
But that they could be my "Lawyers,"
And you would only work for free

I quickly thought it over
And then quickly I agreed
If there was to be a fight ahead
I wanted you to work with me

It seemed we shared the same page
Almost from the start
What's the common law of PA?
My "attorneys" would have no part

They promised they'd work hard for me
The UFT would pay
Ten months have passed; what was done?
Now to me they seem afraid

When they got paid, they asked for more
They ignored my pain and the hurt I bore
I was disillusioned by the whole legal clan
And if it wouldn't hurt me, alone I'd prefer to stand

But unlike many others
Who would be caught totally unaware
I still have you, my Advocate
And I'm thankful you still care

The time spent on this case
And the time you're spending still
If you're not yet sorry you've gotten involved
It must now seem a bitter pill

You now have a crazy job
Combined with an insane attitude
Some think that you're annoying
Others think you're just plain rude

I can see your dedication
I know you're honest and sincere
And though you are persistent
You don't understand the word fear

You won't ever let me thank you
You always say it's wrong
And if I try to help you somehow
You won't ever go along

Sometimes I see you grouchy
I've seen you angry, bossy or crude
But I've been there, done that
And I still have a rotten attitude

And now my crazy Advocate
I have one last thing to say
I'm glad that you and I are friends
I hope that friends we'll always stay

My Dancing Partner

By Francine Skye Lentini
7/21/02

We began our life together
As we began our first dance
Clinging to one another
Very glad we took a chance

So why is it so hard to be here?
You would think at first glance
That I would love to be dancing
Since we always loved to dance

But somehow it doesn't feel right
Without you by my side
Some folks asked me to get up
To dance the "electric slide"

They remembered that we did it well
But they forgot we then were two
And when I heard the music play
I remembered dancing with you

People kept asking me
Why don't you get up to dance?
Even though I was at a wedding
I was afraid to take a chance

To get up to dance without you
And to think you should be there
How could I dance without Blu?
To all those country songs we shared

So I sat quietly at my table
Remembering you always by my side
And I felt you whispering in my ear
"I love you, my little Skye"

Then as the song "Unforgettable"
Really took me by surprise
I realized I've been on empty
Since the fateful day you died

Now I'm left without you
You'll never hold me anymore
The next time I'll dance with you
Will be at Heaven's door

So my Darlin' Jack E Blu
As my heart emits a sigh
You'll always be my dancing partner
Even if only in my mind

My Rotten Attitude

By Francine Skye Lentini
7/24/02

What am I doing here among all this rubble
Between my lawyers and my advocate
I'm always in trouble
I long for peace from this long ordeal
An end in sight would be a good deal

I hate all these things that I have to go through
To get the recognition that we once knew
Now getting through each day is so dreary
Without you by my side I feel so damned weary

I know you would want me to go on with this plight
I know you would want to protect me and my rights
I've been hurt, disrespected, disillusioned and deprived
And the pain that's inside me makes it hard to survive

I hate being bothered by all the details
The litigation, the decisions;
These intrusions won't let me heal
Now heartless, and hopeless and betrayed I feel
Like nothing is comforting and nothing is real
My family and friends still try their best
But the feelings inside me remain so depressed
There is little to be done, it's plain enough to see
As I watch my life in shambles, crumbling around me

And no one is around to soothe or comfort me
Or to say everything will be all right,
Just you wait and see
It used to be you, who would comfort and soothe
Now it's only me left alone, with my rotten attitude

It Was Only Yesterday

By Francine Skye Lentini
7/25/02

It was only yesterday
Yet it seems so far away
When we lived our life together
Without the pain I feel today
Emotions were so steady
So loving, and so aware
Now they're stifled
They're sorrowful
And sometimes even scared

It was only yesterday
When I awoke beside you
Your warm and loving body
Your uplifting attitude
It was hard to feel badly
With you always by my side
You were my friend, my husband
My counselor, my guide

It was only yesterday
We would get away
As you drove, we talked all night
About our work, about our day

It was only yesterday
When we planned and schemed

To sell our house
To buy "big" land
And to retire to our dreams
We were going to find the cowboys
The one's you said were real
You said if we went out west
We'd see them riding in the fields

It was only yesterday
You said you had lots of work to do
"Come kiss me my little caffeine junkie"
Then you said, "I love you!"

It was only yesterday
That you took the train
To your Tower number two
Where you worked to save the others
And no one there could save you

It was only yesterday
That I cried, as they laid you in the ground

And it was only yesterday
The beginning of existence without you around

And it was only yesterday
The unbearable pain broke my heart in two

And now its today
And my life's still empty without you

Your Memorial

By Francine Skye Lentini
8/5/02

You wanted to plant a Christmas tree
And to decorate it too
But last fall came and we all wept
You had God's work to do

Now that a year has come and gone
I plan to take you home
To the place you loved the most on earth
To our BluSkye Ranch you'll roam

There I will plant that tree for you
For all the world to see
I will place the cross Joe made in front
To mark the place you'll always be

Father Vito will say a special Mass
Where many prayers we'll read
Then we'll all gather around the yard
To watch the planting of your tree

Our friends and family will join us
To welcome you as you come home
They will share some of their memories
And special times with you they'd known

And in the ground beneath your tree
 I will place your WTC urn
And with it I'll place your glasses
That you might now want returned

An angel will stand in front of it
To protect you through the night
And above your tree a light will shine
To keep your place so bright

And there our friends will lay a stone
A special tribute it will be
To say if I could I'd climb to heaven
To bring you home with me

And your life will be remembered
By all of us throughout all time
May you rest in peace at BluSkye Ranch
Our home; both yours and mine

A Sad Year

By Francine Skye Lentini
8/6/02

September eleventh the world crashed down
In October the remains of your body were found
November on Thanksgiving I tried hard to pray
December our birthdays were too hard to take

January arrived and the New Year did start
Unemployed still from the pain in my heart
February Valentine's Day made my heart break
Thinking of my lost love keeping me awake

March was your birthday, and I cried all day
April brings renewal is what they say
I felt your absence on Easter and I prayed
I felt myself longing for you all day

Mother's Day, as always, was in the month of May
I missed your flowers and the things you used to say
June was Father's Day, and my dad's birthday too
Father's Day I cried the whole night through

Then I began writing poems as I thought of you

July was my first trip to Pennsylvania this year
Without your company, I felt empty, lonely, and scared
Though the whole family came to support me in our
        home

Even among all of them, I still felt all alone

August was Mom's birthday, and your flowers she
    missed
I brought her some, but they were delivered without
    your kiss
Now September is upon us and your anniversary will
    appear
And this heartache I'm feeling will elevate I fear

With the pictures, the stories, the grief so severe
Upon remembering these things my breath will
    disappear
Forcing me to relive the terror of that clear September
    day
When the terrorists came to America and tore you
    away

Where I'm At

By Francine Skye Lentini
8/27/02

My support system seems to be crumbling
Much like my emotions are doing to me
I'll tell you just what I'm feeling
So you might see just what I see

The people they came and they clamored
When the World Trade Center came tumbling down
"How are you?" "Did they find Jack?"
(I heard them constantly)
Family and friends kept coming around
"What can we do?" "How can we help?"
(Another familiar sound)

I had no answer
I was silent
In agony and confused
The crowds kept screaming around me
"Tell us what to do!"

I had no answer, watched TV
Watched Towers fall and cried
I looked at people running 'round
The smoke from hell was wild

My phone kept ringing off the hook
(Friends and family called)

"Where is Jack?"
"How are you?"
"Placed his picture on the walls?"

Weeks went by without any news
Friends and family stayed
Keeping vigil by my side
They prayed both night and day

They brought me food; told me to eat
To never give up hope
Days passed into weeks
Hope sank, it didn't float

Jack was found; he was ID'd
By needles of his blood
He was buried in the ground
I crumbled without his love

Friends and family still came by
Or they called me every day
"Be strong"
"Life goes on"
"Time heals"
Are all the things they'd say

I took my leave, I struggled on
Family and friends still at my side
I volunteered I made new friends
"Thank God, *you* are alive"

I spoke to priests, I spoke to therapists
And saw a psychiatrist or two

They said, "Go on"
They said, "Be strong"
"Take some pills"
"Life starts anew"

Well now a year has almost gone
And still it's here I sit
I still can't work
To "teach" is out
For my "kids," I am not fit

When I ask my friends to visit
They now have work to do
One has her health to worry her
Another has to move

Another's life is upside down
With choices she must face
A sister's home from the hospital
With bruises on her face

A son is asking, "Go back to school?"
"Could you check this out for me?"
Another sister's on vacation
Like Jack and I would be

My parent's home is worked on
While they wait, they dread the mess
Joe across the street is crying
Rose's memory causes him unrest

My neighbors when they see me
Ask when will I go back to work

They're thinking I'm just plain lazy
I should go on
Why should I still hurt?

The phone calls have slowed down now
It's Chris or me they're looking for
But not the me who is of present
The me who I was before

The me that could easily conquer
All obstacles put in my way
The me that could solve all your problems
That you brought to me every day

The me who could settle a difference
The me that could end a dispute
The me that never cried easily
Ask me and you'd get the truth

It's almost a year since it happened
It's almost a year to the day
When the me that people remember
Crumbled and lost her own way

I stood by the locker room window
With other teachers standing around
One said "Thank God we know no one
In the Towers; they're falling down"

The old me screamed
"Why don't you listen?"
The old me said
"My husband's in there!"

The new me just started screaming
Grabbed my bag and ran down the stairs

The new me now faces returning
To a place where I saw it all
To the school's locker room window
Forcing me to relive their fall

So now I tell you who surround me
Who think that the new me has gone
Do you know how wrong you are now?
I still don't know how to go on

Yes, I still go through all the motions
Of living my life every day
I eat, never sleep, then I shower
I walk, then I talk, then I pray

But the grief that has overwhelmed me
Now it's almost a year
Still hurts me with each day's new dawning
The old me has not yet appeared

The days when laughing was easy
(In those days, living was too)
It just seems to keep getting harder
I'm still hurting and still missing Blu

I hope that you now realize
Try to listen when you talk to me
Understand I'm still struggling with living
And I'm not where I think I should be

I Love You For Your Heart

By Francine Skye Lentini
8/28/02

He was the kind of man
Who loved best with his heart
I loved that trait about him
He won me from the start

He could make me laugh or smile
He could make the rain go way
But if he made me cry
He was sadder than I
Because my smile had gone away

He would tell me that he loved me
I was his cowgirl Skye
He called me "L'il Darlin'
He loved my "reddish-brown eyes"
To keep a smile on my face
He said was his only goal
He promised to love me forever
With his whole heart and soul

We had our plans just waiting
For our futures yet to come
We spent hours scheming

Hours planning
And hopelessly in love

When I asked Jack why he loved me
And why he never tried to seek
A younger one
A cuter one
His reply came naturally,
"I don't love you for your body
Nor do I love you for your mind
I think that both are lovely
But they're not the reason "why"
Its not because you're beautiful
And I love you're smiling face
And it isn't for your intelligence
Or your deeply rooted faith"

"The reason that I love you
And have loved you from the start
Is the same reason my love's forever,
I love you for your heart"
So now my loving cowboy
My beloved Jack-E-Blu
Know I loved you for your heart, as well
And that I always will

The Counselor: Me

By Francine Skye Lentini
8/31/02

I've always been a counselor
Before, and as Jack's wife
People always asked for my opinion
They all came for my advice

I always found it easy
I solved problems by the score
But since I lost you on 9/11
I can't help them any more

It is impossible to counsel others
Or to tell them what to do
My insides are still quivering
From the shock of losing you

I don't know how to live now
I don't know if I'm insane
I only know to those around me
I must not seem the same

When people come around now
I can't tell them what to do
I can't begin to tell them
How I changed since losing you

I haven't been to work yet
I put volunteering aside
I can't find peace or comfort now
No matter how I try

I've been to therapists and doctors
I still don't know what to do
Take the meds, or try another
My life meaningless without you

You were the counselors' counselor
You planned our future and our life
While I was busy counseling others
I came to you for wise advice

Now the people all around me
Still ask me what I think
They still expect a helpful answer
From the advice of their old "shrink"

No one seems to get it
I just am not the same
The advice that I will give them
Will be different and may sound strange

I can only advise from my experience
I only look at how I handle strife
I only counsel from perspectives
That I've gained throughout my life

And now the pain I'm feeling
Since your devastating loss
Has changed me irrevocably
No one feels how deep my loss

To live my life without my counselor
My friend, my husband, by my side
I now find it hard to counsel
When I think, I start to cry

Maybe some day I will be better
If I can find my way through the pain
Maybe one day I will even counsel
But I will never be the same

Why Write?

By Francine Skye Lentini
8/31/02

Something overcomes me
In the middle of the night
Or when I'm in the shower
Or just dealing with my life
It's this feeling words are jumping
Across the clouds found in my mind
And they cross, they pop, they repeat
Until the right words come in time
It seems as if someone's saying
I have something for you to say
I don't feel like they come from me
But words spill out anyway
Sometimes I know not what I'm writing
And my pen can't seem to stop
I must write down the words
But the words are from the heart

Sometimes they make no sense
To anyone but me
Sometimes they give me solace
Sometimes they give me grief
Sometimes I don't want to write them
Sometimes I feel confused
But the words keep falling about me
Even words I did not choose
It's like the words take my life over

Until I sit and write them down
Like someone is in my head
And scattering his thoughts around
And I am just the instrument
He uses to express
What's going on inside my soul
And causing me unrest

Sometimes others read them
Then they turn to me and say
How could you write so beautifully?
You have important things to say
Have you ever thought of publishing?
Maybe writing a book would help
So many others in your position
Could feel these words as well
So many others are still crying
So many others are feeling pain
So many others can't express it
You could write for all of them
And maybe when they read it
A familiar chord will sound
About their raw emotions
Since the Towers crumbled down
Maybe others understand them
More than you could know
Maybe these words could help them
Maybe that's why you write it so

I'd love to write them for that reason
To console others would be the best
But I write them 'cause words are jumping
And they're causing me unrest

I write it because they're screaming
From the far recesses of my mind
"If you don't put us down now
You'll never find the time"
And if we words reach others
Then all of us would be
Happy to reach those suffering
Throughout all eternity"

Some Days

By Francine Skye Lentini
8/31/02

Some days it just hits me
You're not coming home
Some days I really feel it
Very lonely and all alone
Some days I choose something
And it only reminds me of you
Some days I look around
Wondering what I should do

Some days go very slowly
Without much to pass
Some days I feel tired
Not knowing how to last
Some days I feel lost
No matter who's around
Some days I can't believe it's true
The World Trade Center did come down

Some days it seems impossible
To live through one more day
Some days September eleventh
Haunts me still and I'm afraid
Some days I think I'll make it
I'll try to live again
Some days I keep asking
"Begin to live," and when?

Some days it feels hopeless
Why try to find my way?
Some days I just spend crying
Is there a better way?
Some days I talk to others
They understand? Guide?
Some days I spend in silence
Keeping sorrow deep inside

Some days it feels like yesterday
With your love right next to me
Some days it feels I've suffered
This must be eternity
Some days I feel thankful
For having another day
Some days I feel angry
Asking God "Why must I stay!"

Some days I feel selfish
I won't share my heart
Some days it's broken
It's still tearing me apart
Some days I help others
To try to keep myself sane
Some days I say, "Who cares?"
They have themselves to blame"

Some days I wonder
What am I living for?
Some days I hear Him saying
You have to work a little more

Some days I think enough now
I need an end in sight
Some days I think, never
My life won't ever be right

Some days I wake up thinking
I don't know what I'll do
And some days Our Lord just answers
"Feel my love, and start anew"

My Counselor

(Dedicated to Edward Khusid)
By Francine Skye Lentini
9/2/02

It's nearly a year ago I went, to get some advice from
    him
To lean on his capable shoulders, when grief attacked
    from within
The first time he saw me I could only sit and cry
I couldn't say that much to him, so he looked into my
    eyes

He began by consoling me, through the pain I could not
    bear
He advised me that I could live through it all, even
    though I was scared
He told me what to do right then, and he told me what
    to say
He prepared me for the wake, and he explained to me
    the way

And even for the funeral he laid a simple, yet brilliant
    plan
He said stay close to family and friends and hold tightly
    to their hands
And when the service was over, I should go home
    straight away

Eat something, drink some wine, relax, and eat some
    cake

I knew he was a special counselor right from the very
    start
He made hard things seem simple; he tried to ease my
    heart
I knew that he had patience; he needed a lot for me
I seem to keep repeating things throughout my
    therapy

Sometimes I throw him problems that I still have to
    face
I find him listening avidly with an intense look upon his
    face
I do most of the talking and explain my thoughts to
    him
But he'll interject his sound advice every now and then

Occasionally he tells me I don't know how far I've
    come
I return my answer; "I'm still confused, depressed,
    undone"
I tell him how the thoughts I feel still take a hold of me
He advised me, "Write it down," to help aid my therapy

Several months had passed by and then one night in
    June
I couldn't sleep because I cried, and with pen in hand it
    moved
All the thoughts that I can't say, got written down
    instead

And then I kept on writing; six poems that night in bed

I brought the poems to my counselor the following afternoon
He was impressed, said I am wise, and enjoyed my troubled views
So I kept writing things I felt about everything around
I wrote about Jack E Blu, 9/11, and the Towers falling down

On occasions rare and very few my therapist had to go
To help his wife, to do some duty, for solidarity, he told
And sometimes crises would arise and he would not be there
I'd miss his consoling kindness; without his wisdom, I despaired

And when he returned, we'd continue, to try to ease my grief
We'd talk, I'd cry, he'd listen, and sometimes I'd repeat
My counselor still reminds me that I've come a long, long way
From the day that he first saw me, and I didn't know what to say
He says I give myself no credit for the things that I have done
He says give it time, I will heal, and in time even have some fun

But my kind and caring counselor, always seems to
  know what's best
God blessed me with a counselor that could help me
  through this mess
I thank God that He found him and assigned him right
  to me
If I didn't have his wisdom, only God knows where I'd
  be

All Alone

By Francine Skye Lentini
9/8/02

Last night I sat in my basement
And tried to write a poem
All of a sudden I was crying
I never felt so alone

As I sat there I began to realize
That in only four more days
It would be the year's anniversary
Of when you passed away

It wasn't that you had been sick
Nor by accident were you gone
It was by Hate's devilish finger
That brought the Towers down

There was no rhyme or reason
As to why you went away
You said I'll see you later Skye
Before you went to work that day

You said you had to go in early
Because you had lots of work to do
Little did you know
That day's work was planned for you

The work you had intended
Was not the work you did
You had to help the others
So they could escape and live

You didn't hesitate a moment
When the Lord gave you His call
To be one of his angels
And to give to Him your all

You were always my hero darling
My cowboy tried and true
But now you're not here with me
And I need my angel Blu

I'm trying hard to go on without you
I still need you by my side
But as the day draws near
I just think of you and cry

I think of how you sacrificed
You gave your all that day
And now it's already one whole year
From the day you passed away

And though I believe in Heaven
And I know that's where you'll be
I still have to live my life on earth
Without your precious company

You know some days I feel it
The pain of grief too hard to bear

I keep asking why did you have to go
I feel you everywhere

And I know I have to live
At least for this–a brand new day
But I can't grasp how to do it
Since you have gone away

I feel my life has no purpose
I don't feel like your Skye
I just feel so sad and lonely
I miss you and I cry

The people all around me
Think that I don't even try
They say be strong
You must go on
It's time to dry your eyes

But every time I think of you
I also think of me
I just can't figure it out
How can I be what I used to be?

I feel so alone and so helpless
I don't know how to live my life
Please ask the Lord when you see him
I'm desperate for His loving advice

I know He has the answer
I pray for guidance in my life
Please tell Him Skye is lost here
And she is suffering as your wife

I'm still so far from heaven
When I will see your smiling face
As you welcome me into your loving arms
At Heaven's pearly gate

I don't know when God will call me
But I only pray to God it's true
That someday we will join in Heaven
When Skye will be joined with her Blu

Three Wishes

By Francine Skye Lentini
9/9/02

If God gave me three wishes
I know what the first would be
To allow me into heaven
So I could take you home with me

My second wish is harder
Because I'd never let you go
I'd wish our love eternal
Ne'er to fade like embers glow

Then last I'd wish for more time
For me to share with you
To share peace and love together
In Blu Skye Ranch we'd start anew

Tuesday, 9/10/02

By Francine Skye Lentini
9/10/02

Today is Tuesday the tenth of September 2002
It's one year to the day that I lost you
The actual date 9/11 would be
But it was on a Tuesday that you had to leave

Last year on Tuesday I was in school
The first call came; It couldn't be true
How could a plane hit your tower so high?
A permanent landscape of the New York sky

And then as I watched another plane came
It hit the second Tower; debris began to rain
As this "science fiction" horror began to unfold
I unbelievingly watched the Twin Towers implode

And inside Tower Two, on the 80th floor
My husband saved others; people by the score
But when he tried to save himself, it was too late
For God had planned for him a different fate

He was invited by our Lord to Heaven's door
Where the angels awaited and His glory he saw
At home I still awaited his call in vain
Little did I know I would never see him again

Now tomorrow the eleventh will mark one year
Without you my love who I still hold so dear
Now only my memories, my heartaches remain
I wait for the time when I'll feel less pain

Now when I pray to you to speak to God for me
I ask you to ask God for His holy mercy
To bring an end to this everlasting pain
To allow me to live, and laugh, and feel again
To mend my heart which is broken inside
To remind me of things that make life worthwhile
So Jack tonight as I pray to thee
Please ask our Lord for peace for me

The Anniversary, 9/11/02

By Francine Skye Lentini
9/11/02

The day that I've dreaded is finally here
You've been gone my darling for one whole year
The Anniversary of that day has finally come through
The day I've been agonizing, reliving, missing you

The day I found out your body was found
Among the rubble of that hallowed ground
Is the day that I stopped breathing and the day that I
    cried
For my heart broke in pieces when I learned you died

I haven't been able to go on with my life
My life is different since I last was your wife
No doctors or therapists or those who have tried
Could make me feel comfort; this grief I can't hide

And the pain in my heart is as real today
As the pain that I felt on that cold October day
When police came; they knocked on the door
With the news of you; you are here no more

I couldn't breathe then as I cannot breathe now
The pain deep inside me only I can avow

For me to go back to my life as it was
Without happiness and joy of your all consuming love

This morning when I looked at a rose by my sink
A thought came of you and I started to think

I stared at the petals and said with some doubt
"He loves me (yes)......He loves me not"
Then as I watched a single petal dropped

I somehow sensed what you wanted to say
You love me still even though you're away
As I stared at that rose I started to cry
I will love you too until the day that I die

I wish you a Happy Anniversary in heaven, my love
I dream of seeing you one day in heaven above
And until that day when we can start anew
I will go on forever still loving you

Our Love

By Francine Skye Lentini
9/14/02

People often tell me that I shouldn't be so sad
Instead I should feel lucky for the special love we
    shared
People also tell me what they would do to have one day
To be in love like me and you; I turn to them and say:
We loved each other for our hearts; we both loved so
    fine
We always thought of the other first; what was yours,
    was also mine
We loved to spend all of our time, together if we could
We shared the same likes and dreams; plans we made
    were good
We danced together, worked together, and always
    volunteered
We walked together, we talked things over, and we slept
    like cuddly bears
Everyone who saw us said that they knew just by a
    glance
That we were perfect together and that our love was
    sure to last
People who never had such a love now look at me and
    say
You don't know how lucky you are; I was never loved
    that way
But what they cannot realize, and perhaps they never
    will

Is that you can't miss what you never had, the way that
I miss you

Invisible

By Francine Skye Lentini
9/14/02

Sometimes I feel invisible
Can anyone see me?
Do they know how I feel?
Can they feel my agony?

Sometimes I feel invisible
Am I getting in the way?
Am I a problem you're trying to solve?
Do you know me for today?

Sometimes I feel invisible
Like I don't know where I am
Like I don't know how to do it
How to make a future plan

Sometimes I feel invisible
One half of me is gone
Only one half is still remaining
And that half can't go on

Sometimes I feel invisible
I don't even have to hide
No one sees me anyway
It's hard to laugh when tears collide

Sometimes I feel invisible
Like I'm not even here
Like when I speak no one hears me
It's as if I've disappeared

Sometimes I think being invisible
Is not such a bad way to be
No one talks to you at all
No one listens attentively

And if sometimes I do call someone
And nobody answers on the line
It doesn't bother me at all; I still feel just fine
Because by being invisible
I'm finally able...
To rest this weary mind

My Wandering Mind

By Francine Skye Lentini
9/17/02

The thoughts that run in and out of my mind are very
real
I remember us doing so many things; it's the little
things I feel
Tonight I thought of how you would love this memorial
I planned
You always wanted family and friends to picnic on our
Promised Land

So isn't it ironic that it's happening this year
You can only join us in spirit, because you're no longer
here
All who are coming have the highest respect for you
They're coming from all directions just to say a prayer
or two

Though you've proved you were a hero on that saddest
day of all
It's still hard for us to understand why you were a
chosen soul
The only answer we came up with, as we were pondering
this
Is that God needed another Angel aboard his "Saving"
ship

When I picture all of our loved ones joining us to pray

I hope that you'll be near me, when "thank you," is all
 I'll say
But my darlin' love, my sweetheart, my cowboy Jack E
 Blu
The love we shared just must go on, because it was
 forever tried and true

And sometimes if you see me reading your cards and
 starting to cry
Could you let me know you're next to me, by wiping the
 tears from my eyes
You could always make it better, and cheered me up on
 many days
You had that special knack about you, with your
 unpredictable crazy ways

And something that keeps occurring to me, now that a
 year has passed
Is that you're still around, you're coming home, your
 loss I can't get past

There have been times in my life when I lived alone
 with Chris, my son
I always knew that I could make it; I could do it on my
 own
But in our seven years together, you've shown me how
 life could be
How two could be better than one; and life could be
 sweeter as three

Now I just wrestle with the question "How do I get
    along?"
Without my country cowboy singing to me his country
    songs
Now your cards are missing when a holiday appears
And all the love you poured inside, is now gone, it's
    disappeared

So although I've been alone before, and I handled it
    well, in truth
Now I feel lonely all the time instead, and there's
    nothing I can do
I wish you could still come here to comfort me like you
    used to do

My biggest wish is very simple, even though it can't
    come true
I wish I could hold you in my arms once more and say
    goodnight to you

Why Does God...?

By Francine Skye Lentini
9/18/02

"If there's a God, how could this happen?"
I've heard many skeptics say
Every time something goes awry
Or someone doesn't get his way
Or when things in life aren't right
Or when some tragedy occurs
Or whenever a loved one dies
We ask, "Where's God, if pain endures?"

Why does suffering combat man?
Why do we go to war?
Why do mothers labor in pain?
Why are some children ignored?
Why do parents turn their backs?
Why does pornography entertain?
Where is God the skeptics sing?
If He were here we'd have no pain

If there's a God where was He
When the World Trade Center fell?
Why did he not stop the tragedy?
This insanity fraught from hell?

I have no answer to what others ask
I cannot explain the Lord's way
It doesn't have to make sense right now
He has nothing to explain

No one can know these answers now
We ask our questions in vain
Yet while we're living here on earth
Only God knows destiny's hand

A plan was written before our birth
We were given the freedom to expand
To bear the crosses and the hurts
The pain and suffering that is at hand

Even this we can't compare
To the suffering of our Lord
To save us from Evil's lair
His own crucifixion he endured

Now we are asked to live our best
And to trust in God's own plan
And if all of our questions can't be answered now
This too we're asked to understand

If we want to deserve a place with God
When we say our final prayers
We must accept our crosses now
And whatever we're asked to bear

BluSkye Ranch Memories

By Francine Skye Lentini
9/20/02

You've been on my mind this whole day, today
From the time I awoke, until the time I prayed
Every room I walked through and on every wall
Is a memory I shared with you that I love to recall

I remember the first night here we slept right here on
the floor
The next day we signed papers that made the house
mine and yours
I thought of the dreams and the plans that we shared
How so many came true; many others still planned

I remember how crazy buying furniture had been
I dragged you through Pennsylvania; you always made
me win
Then we planned the extension, Dad, you, and me
With it's walls, insulation, floor, and ceiling

And I remember the cracked molding; you said you'd
try to fool Dad
But the joke was on you when he said, "What did you
do Jack?"

When the extension was finished and Dad was
  satisfied
We said let's have Thanksgiving and invite the whole
  tribe

The family slept in every room in the house
On the beds, on the floor and on the pull-out couch
I woke up at 6AM to put the turkey in
But by 11:30AM the lights went dim

We cooked on the propane stove
As we struggled hard to see
But as we prayed our Thanksgiving prayers
The lights returned and lit up everything

Later, with Mom and Dad, we'd decorate our Christmas
  tree
Then we'd decorate the house for the entire world to
  see
We left the lights on timers so that every night they'd
  glow
To wish a Merry Christmas-to even those we didn't
  know

But what we always said we wanted was a real Christmas
  tree
We planned to put it in our yard; you said it was for me
Now soon we will plant that tree for you my shining
  star
And I will light it every year for our neighbors near and
  far

I know that you had to leave that fateful September
day
But I wish you were able to see our plan as it comes true
today
May God grant you a little time off so that you could
see
The fulfillment of your promise when we plant our
Christmas tree

I still love you, I still miss you, and I still long for you
each day
And every memory we made at BluSkye Ranch will here
forever stay

One Week Away

By Francine Skye Lentini
9/21/02

The special day I've been planning is one week away
The Memorial for you will be held on Saturday
The 28th of September will remain in my mind
As a holiday for you, my hero, who was courageous and
     kind

You always were a kidder, and could always get me
     good
It took me years to catch on; and I only rarely could
I ordered a big tent, tables, chairs and lights
For 50 of our loved ones to celebrate your life

I ordered trays of cold cuts, rolls, and desserts too
And Father Vito will say a mass in memory of you
We'll have programs and flowers and prayers will be
     said
But the fact still remains, I can't believe that you're
     dead

My mind still can't accept that you are no longer here
And in time I must accept the fact that I'm without you
     near
Every room, every picture, every leaf on every tree
Brings back memories of you when you were here with
     me

It's over a year and yet I still grieve
When I realize you're gone; it's like a bad dream
The only thing worse is, I know it's true
I have to go on living my life here without you

And though I'm making this memorial for you and you
    alone
It feels like a sort of celebration of you coming home
To live in BluSkye Ranch was our future dream
Now my heart is breaking because you're not here with
    me

But when I place the WTC ashes beneath your Blue
    Spruce tree
I'll find peace knowing that you're where you want to
    be
I know you hated Staten Island, yet that is where your
    body rests
I always knew you'd rather lie in the place you loved the
    best

When on July 17th, 1997, we bought our BluSkye ranch
We never dreamt, we never thought, that in only four
    years you'd pass

When I look at the wooden shingle we hung on the wall
    outside
I remember how we were so happy and our hearts just
    burst with pride
We christened our home with its name on that happy
    July day
And the name we chose, "BluSkye Ranch," is the name
    that will always stay

Next week we'll all honor you for your courage and
    dignity
And I'll be the proudest of all, when we plant your Blue
    Spruce tree

Though others will see this only as a memorial that is
    your due
I will see it as a dream; one we hoped would come true
I know we'll be together forever, in this place we both
    loved
Even though I'm here alone and you're in heaven above

I hope you can be here with us on the day we honor
    you
And that you'll be smiling down at us, My Darlin'
    Cowboy Blu

Are We Ready?

By Francine Skye Lentini
9/22/02

Today I was busy with a lot of things to do
Mom and Dad were here and they worked hard too
We finished the cleaning, the shopping, the chores
We didn't leave anything out; of that we're very sure
We think we're now ready, your memorial is due
Soon it will be Saturday and all will honor you
We want it to be holy; a celebration of your life
The yard is all ready; your tree is just right
The electric we asked our handyman to do
He said it would be finished before the week is through
Tonight we went out for dinner when our work was
        done
We came home so tired, that only Kari could run
But while we ate dinner, my mom and dad and me
I told them both how incredible all of this still seems
I know that you're gone now for more than a year
But I still can't help feeling that you're around me here
My mom said I should not cry and should try to
        understand
That you went straight to Heaven, as a hero of a man
And she said we were taught that Heaven would always
        be
More beautiful and perfect than anything we've seen
She said that of course you are deeply missed
But nothing compares to our dear Lord's blessed kiss
So my love of my life, My Jack E Blu, I pray

That all goes perfectly for this your Memorial Day
The hardest thing so far that I've ever had to do
Is to learn how to live again, here on earth without you

Welcome Home Jack E Blu

By Francine Skye Lentini
10/1/02

Welcome home my dearest Blu
You're back at the Ranch with me
I'm so proud of the life you lived
And how you died heroically

Our friends and family all worked so hard
To see this dream come true
I returned you to our BluSkye Ranch
Like you would have wanted me to do

The yard looks so lovely now
With your blue spruce tree
Joe's cross is in front of it
While your angel stands and gleams

A memorial stone was placed by Monica and Ron
The words upon it are very true
They say if I could, I'd climb to heaven
So that I could be with you

Mike did a portrait
I laid four special stones
Barbara did a beautiful program
And included my memorial poem

Skip and Sharon brought us flowers
Joe and Barbara brought a bench
Jaime and Carmine brought candles
To fill the air with their sweet scents

Jackie and Anthony brought a book
A keepsake and a candle for the day
In it I will place all the memories
So that they may never fade

I had a special box
In which I placed your urn
I added a little pair of cowboy boots
A cowboy hat
A Yankee charm
And your glasses
All the things I thought you'd like returned
Then I added a program
Before I closed it tight
And I wrapped it in an American flag
To present it, for burial, just right

I removed the flag from the box
Before I placed it in the ground
Then I kissed it and prayed for you
Before Chris poured the soil all around

As Father Vito said your Mass
We all prayed for you
I read my poem, Chris read a bible verse
As Jackie and Anthony J. did too

Daniel taped the entire day

From the Mass to the planting of the tree
He reminded me of you
When you used to tape
All of our special occasions for me

And all of us were happy
As we all honored you
But we all cried, as you were welcomed home
'Cause we're all still missing our Jack E Blu

People Say

By Francine Skye Lentini
10/1/02

People say to move on now
I've been saddened for over a year
It's time to go on with my life
Your spirit will always be near

Some people call me your cowgirl, Skye
Other people call me your wife
But all agree we had it all together
We did our best to enjoy our lives

People know I loved you
People know that you loved me
They say we were like two kids
Who played house and family

People say they never saw two people
Who were so apparently in love
They say that if you just looked at us
We shined brightly, like stars above

People say I should move on now
I should be strong and have some fun
They remind me you're always with me
Even though you're in heaven above

People say to stop my crying
They say my sorrow is in vain
People say love like ours is eternal
And that someday we'll love again

People say a lot of things
But none can comfort or ease my pain
Because people haven't told me yet
How to live till we meet again

A Very Bad Day

By Francine Skye Lentini
October 6, 2002

All I want to say is that I'm having a very bad day
My sister called, my son called and I pushed them all
   away

I don't want to move; I don't want to eat
I just finished ironing, and I plan to go to sleep

To turn off the torture that's running in my mind
The loneliness, the solitude that I cannot define
It feels as if breathing is taking my breath away
I don't want to talk about it; there's nothing I can say

I've said it once; I've said it twice and so many times
   before
How do I go on without your love? I can't say it
   anymore
I'm so tired and I'm so sad, all I want to do is cry
If I didn't believe as I do in Him, I would just lay down
   and die

I know the people around me don't want to talk to me
   anymore
They've all just about had it; Enough of this! That's for
   sure!
To them it's been a year and more since you died that
   September day

To me, I'm just realizing, that you've gone away to stay

My life is so different than anything I've lived before
I have experienced sadness, but this is that and so much
    more

I try to express my feelings; I try to say what I feel
But a lot of what I've been saying, though repetitive, is
    very real

My emotions haven't gone through all that I must feel
To once and for always realize this loss is really real
And that I will not see you on this earth for one more
    day
That you' re now living in Heaven, and that seems so
    very far away

Signs of You

By Francine Skye Lentini
10/7/02

The first day the Towers fell a Mets bear hit me in the
head
It briefly crossed my mind it's you, but then I'd have to
admit you're dead

Then every evening at 6:15, Kari would start to bark
I ran to the window; were you coming home? Could
Kari see what I could not?

Then a package came addressed to you but you still had
not come home
I opened it and looked inside, the gifts inside were to
be my own
I closed the box and put it away, I didn't want to look
inside
If I took the gifts you meant for me, I would have to
admit you'd died

A bill was sent for the gifts received, I called to say you
were gone
After they checked all the facts, they told me to keep
them for my own
So I put them away and decided right then what you
would have wanted me to do
I opened one up on my birthday, and then on Christmas
I opened two

I spent December 6th in Long Island with my sister
    Jacqueline
Close to 12 am, I was riding home and feeling bad for
    me again
I thought of how you always said my birthday should be
    a happy day for me
But I was crying as I was driving home, and telling you
    that couldn't be

Now in my mind I thought I heard you say "Skye it's still
    not time"
That this year you'll start my birthday with a different
    kind if sign
As the clock struck 12, and as I cried, I was driving over
    a hill
And when I reached the other side I saw a sign you
    loved me still
The lights were bright and all aglow and twinkling in
    the night
As if you screamed I couldn't sing, so I lit up the sky

I just remained and thanked you but then thought how
    could I believe
This wasn't a trick played by my mind for me on my
    birthday's eve
A few more times my Mets bear would hit me in the
    head
Sometimes it would fall on the floor
The Yankee bear would be grinning just like you used to
    grin before

Then I remembered other times when you brought
  flowers for me
There was never an occasion; you said love is what they
  are for
You always told me I deserved them because I was so
  true
And I loved you so my darling, because I knew you
  really knew

Then the day of your memorial, to many, there were no
  signs to be seen
But funny how Chris and I noticed a sign you sent to us
  from Kari Okie
You must have been there in spirit, and Kari must have
  heard your call
She was walking around and searching to find you, to
  respond to you for us all

Chris mentioned to me when it was over, that he saw
  what Kari Okie had done
His mind and my mind were together; it was a sign of
  your presence and love
Another sign came through on that weekend; I noticed
  it the weekend before
In some pots that had dirt but no plantings, now little
  flowers they bore
After a week I returned there to notice, to see if those
  flowers still grew
And to my surprise they were blooming, not in one pot,
  but in two

I mentioned this to some friends there; they said that's
  how perennials grow

The come up each year after you plant them, it's not
    unusual, it's just so
What they did not realize, and what they missed I fear
Is impatiens are just annuals, they have to be planted
    every year
And since I never planted them and since they
    blossomed on their own
I accepted them and I thanked you; for giving me
    flowers the day I brought you home

Grief

By Francine Skye Lentini
10/11/02

I am reading a book to learn how a person grieves
It explains a process that one goes through without any
reprieve

It says that if you go on living, like everything is fine
You are only hiding your feelings, which need to be
defined

Grief can be worked through, however painful it must
seem
And if one chooses not to face it, grief can destroy a
person's dreams
The book goes on to explain other options
If you work through it you can transcend

Although grief did have a beginning; it really has no
end
You just learn to incorporate the spirit, in your heart it
has to blend
Though at times it seems impossible to even comprehend

So though one is still grieving it's encouraging to know
One can transcend the insatiable pain and through it
one can grow

The Poetry Circle

By Francine Skye Lentini
10/11/02

I was sitting in a poetry circle, listening to their words
I asked myself why am I here, it seems to be absurd
The others' words seem so wise and so profound
Their vocabulary is superior; all listen without a sound

I listened as an author read from a book he wrote
And the others, many authors too, what feelings they
    evoked!
Their poems were in a special form; they could identify
    each so well
Why am I here among such writers; my poems can't
    compare, pray tell

As each person read his poems, many others closed
    their eyes
To experience the poet's words, without any
    compromise
All were talented and professional with words so
    sincere
So when it came to read my poems, they seemed
    childish, I feared

So as the circle went around, until the one to read was
    me
I was surprised when I was asked to read not one, or
    two, but three!

And after it was over I felt honored even more
Because the authors and the poets told me that I should
  go forth
I should really try to publish, these, my simple poems
So that others in my position, can feel the feelings they
  evoke

I was even offered advice and compliments by two or
  three
I don't think those authors realized what their
  recognition meant to me

BluSkye Limerick

By Francine Skye Lentini
10/13/02

To Blu Skye Ranch every weekend we'd roam
To a piece of Heaven; we made our own
The deer loved their trough
Till Kari Okie barked them off
Then on Sunday we would hate to go home

The Six Senses

By Francine Skye Lentini
10/17/02

I wish I could see your charming smile one more time
I wish I could hear your voice and your laugh on the
line
I wish I could smell that cowboy cologne you used to
spray
I wish I could touch your warm cuddly body, just for
today
I wish I could taste your tender kisses on my longing
lips
And last
I wish I had a sixth sense that could return my man
The man that all my senses miss

A Prayer

By Francine Skye Lentini
10/17/02

A prayer can fly on angel's wings
With a comforting voice it sweetly sings
To describe our feelings deep inside
Until to God's ears it will arrive

Your Loving Poems

By Francine Skye Lentini
10/17/02

I miss the poems you wrote to me
Your thoughts were stated most romantically
Your sensitive feelings you would express
They surrounded my soul with their caress
They made me feel so special, so loved
You put me on a pedestal so high above

The poems you wrote you didn't rhyme
They came in cards you sent
Your additions were so fine
You described in your own words how you felt
Such romantic, touching words that my heart would melt

And though you are now gone, I need you to know
You were my bard of romance, and I loved you so
You always wrote of how I changed your life
And how you couldn't be without me at any price
And then you thanked me for loving you
But my love for you came naturally,
My loving Jack E Blu

Unrelenting Heartache

By Francine Skye Lentini
10/19/02

I know just when it started tonight
As I was sitting in church
I missed you sitting next to me
And my heart began to hurt
I lit two candles before the Mass
I prayed for both our families
I prayed the rosary for you
Still feeling lonely as can be

We went to eat at Carmen's
Just me, my mom and dad
I drank some wine, we talked, and we laughed
Yet still I felt so sad

When we got home I got Kari, and I took her for a
    walk
I walked around with Kari, crying, while to you I
    talked
I told you I was lonely here with you so far away
I told you how I miss you more with each passing day
I told you that I loved you and could you please send
    me a sign
Then I saw a rose peeking through a fence
Was it from you or was it the wine?

I walked along the empty streets
Kari still by my side
But my heart was heavy as we walked
Then finally we went inside

Then my father said he just saw you
Your face was pictured on the screen
They said it was a religious show
They were surprised by what they'd seen
They said they showed the date of birth and the date
    you died
They said I had just missed it, it came on while I was
    outside

I thought again that maybe it was a sign you sent to me
But since I had just missed it, it caused me misery

And now I'm lying in my bed and thinking of when we
    went to church
How you loved singing Amazing Grace, while reading
    all the words
Sometimes you'd touch my pinky; sometimes you
    touched my hair
Sometimes you even held my hand, to show how much
    you cared

Now weekends come and weekends go, and nothing is
the same
And the longer I am without you, the deeper is my
pain
Advice is constantly given
"Take your pills"
"Talk to shrinks"

"Get some sleep; you'll be just fine."
"If you feel like it, with dinner, have some wine"

But honey I feel like I'll never feel happy
I think I will always be blue
I wish I could wish our life back
The way we had it, me and you

The Miracle Is

By Francine Sky Lentini
10/29/02

The miracle is I'm sitting here writing the feelings in
    my heart
On paper in my basement while my clothes are in the
    wash
The miracle is I'm thinking, since you're gone,
    everything is new
The miracle is I'm supposed to start living life, again,
    without you
The miracle is I'm still breathing; it's so long you've
    been away
I always think to tell you something, then I remember
    it's not okay
It's a miracle that I function; I see tomorrow and yearn
    for yesterday
It's a miracle that I get things done and try to think how
    I should live
It's a miracle how I can survive at all, with my heart
    broken as it is
It's a miracle that we had such love, as only we two
    could
It's a miracle we had so little time, but we made our life
    so good
It's a miracle God gives me strength to face each brand
    new day
It hasn't gotten any easier since the time you passed
    away

Now the miracle is I'm living, while you are here no
    more
And now and again I try to remember what am I living
    for?

Write or Not?

By Francine Skye Lentini
10/28/02

I've been told to put my thoughts on paper, to express
    exactly how I feel
How could I begin without saying it-nothing still seems
    for real
How do I start to explain these feelings that are mangled
    around my heart
Sometimes I want to blame you, but you never meant to
    break my heart
And the pain that still sears through it, is just tearing
    me apart

I know that someday I will see you when we meet at
    heaven's door
But right now my feelings are muddled and my soul is
    torn and sore
I now feel nervous and jumpy and anxious all the time
Other times I feel depressed, I cry and my eyes shine
I am tired of all the issues that plague my days and
    nights
I'm so weary, I'm so tired, I have lost my will to fight

Every day's another battle, every week another war
Sometimes I can't imagine what I'm living for
It's not that I'm not thankful for the gifts that God gave
    me
Its' just that I feel so lonely; I need peace and serenity

Grief encompasses my feelings; its' always there, can't
be ignored
Every time I write my thoughts down the pain inside
me hurts some more

I will try to express my feelings as I go on from day to
day
But my writing may seem puzzling because my thoughts
are disarrayed
When I stop to write my poetry, it sometimes feels my
heart will break
Should I continue to write such feelings, though they
cause my soul to ache?

Deep Depression

By Francine Skye Lentini
10/30/02

They say that you are in heaven
But I don't know where that is
Are you like a sparkling star?
Or is your spirit in my midst

Sometimes I think I hear you
In the deep recesses of my mind
When I think I hear you
You tell me I'll be fine

Other times I hear you,
You say "Skye, I'm not 'away' "
Then I hear you say you love me
And will 'til my dying day

Yet when I think it's over
It doesn't seem you went away
I expect to see you walking
Back to me, on any day

I expect I'll hear, "Honey I'm home!"
Like you always used to do
My mind is deeply muddled
As I try to hold on to you

Why am I here? I can't move on
There are chains that bind
My thoughts are in turmoil
With chains of love, I find

And yet a part of me still believes
That life must be more than this
We did find our love on earth
And we found true happiness

The problem now is sadness
I have no pleasures, always pain
I feel adrift in this place called earth
I wanted you here, to always remain

I don't know what I need anymore
Friends and family offer advice
But I still haven't any answer
As to how do I continue my life?

They think that I am just brooding
I am doing this to myself
They tell me I'm strong; move on
But what I feel they never felt

Doesn't anybody get it?
It's so simple for me to see
I never got to say goodbye
Before you had to leave

Even though I saw the Towers fall
Even though I knew you were inside
I cried, and still I waited
With the telephone by my side

There was your wake and funeral
And I had a memorial just for you
I even saw them put you in the ground
In shock, I cried, "It can't be true"

Now I am so tired
I still have to take some pills
Since this depression continues
Others guide me still

Therapists and priests tell me
Take it one day at a time
Go out, keep busy, have fun,
I can't do that, when I'm crying

I can't accept any excuses
This pain is far too real
This depression and this sadness
Is exactly how I feel

Some say if you see me crying
You would turn over in your grave
You always wanted me to be happy
You are my hero and were so brave

They say to throw away the problems
Those that eat me up inside
I passed them over to my advocate
Now she has the control and offers advice

I think what you would want for now
Was what you wanted for me in life
But it still leaves me to wonder
At what cost, is this merciless plight?

So I still do not know how to recover
I still don't even "see the light"
I feel I am not myself anymore
And I can't sleep at night

I'm too stressed to figure this out now
I wish you could tell me what to do
What are the answers to all of my questions?
Do I really need another's point of view?

So here I sit writing my poetry
Like an empty shell in an unending sea
And I'm still wondering, where can I find you?
I need your help and your prayers for me

My Mom and Dad

By Francine Skye Lentini
11/10/02

My mom and dad are married
Now, for more than 54 years
And every time I think of it
My eyes fill up with tears
I don't know how they did it
They can't believe it too
But I could attest to their lasting love
As I am turning fifty-two
When my friends ask me their ages
I tell them because I'm so proud
They say they look much younger
They must stand out from their crowd

They stand out in so many ways
I can't begin to count
But I'll start with saying, "Thank you God"
For the parents You picked me out
They've been the heart of our family
We all stand together side by side
And when one of us is suffering
It's all of us who cry

But the point I'm trying to make here
Is that I am so full of pride
That my parents are still going strong
And remain always by my side

I have had a tough time of it
Since September 11th, 2001
And they stuck right there by my side
And called Jack E Blu their son
My Dad and he were buddies
Each breaking the other's chops
My mom would love the flowers
And his kind words from his heart

And I know their hearts are breaking
Right along with mine
And I know how sad I make them
Seeing me struggling to survive
No words can quite describe them
I will love them throughout my life
And if my fondest prayer be answered
They will live forever, by my side

This poem is dedicated to my Mom and Dad,
With all my love

Agonizing Still

By Francine Skye Lentini
11/15/02

I walked the dog around by the cemetery tonight
And as always said the same prayer
Lord please have mercy on the souls buried here
And on the souls that I hold so dear
And especially on my husband, my love so true
My own true hero, Jack E Blu

All of a sudden tonight I couldn't believe it
I asked myself why am I saying this prayer
I suddenly felt overwhelmed with grief
And it all came back so painfully clear

I still feel you must be here
You can't have passed away
We should be spending weekends in PA.
And we should be leaving every Friday

And then it finally hit me
I've been saying this same prayer
Every time I walked the dog
Passed that old cemetery this year
And how my life has changed
From feeling so happy to feeling so blue
Because it's still hard for me to take the pain
Of living without you

I never met another man prouder of me than you
You said we would never part
I believed it to be true
And I know you don't want to see me cry
But I don't understand the evil ones
And why so many had to die

I can't imagine what you went through
When you realized it was time
Were you frightened?
Were you crying?
Were you praying?
Or were you asking why?

When it finally happened, did it happen very fast?
Did you suffer pain and agony, while you waited and
    time passed?

As you went up to help the others
Something you volunteered to do
Did you fear that you could be trapped?
With no stairways left to use?
Were you panicked by the thought that you might not
    be saved?
And in your final moments, did you see the Lord's
    blessed face?

As I think of these things I agonize
About what you must have went through
And how I wish I could have been there
To hold you close and comfort you

Now I have only your memory

And I still feel so much pain
When they say that love's forever
Is that beyond our present time frame?

If God is Love as I've been taught, and if He is
everywhere
I trust in Him and believe someday, we'll be united in
His care
So my darling Jack E Blu please pray that I recover in
time
I will always be your Lil' Darling, and forever you'll be
mine

Lonely vs. Alone

By Francine Skye Lentini
11/24/02

There is a big difference
Between the words 'lonely' and 'alone'
One implies you are by yourself
The other says you feel forlorn
You can be alone and be happy
You may have many things to do
But when you're lonely and feeling desolate
You're often depressed and feeling blue
You can be lonely with people around you
Because loneliness comes from within
Just because you're with people
Few know the pain that you're in
I have been alone before
Many times in my past
Between some relationships
That weren't meant to last
I never felt as I feel now
Such a sickness in my heart
I don't know how I'm living
Since the day you had to part
Our relationship required nothing
We just knew how well it worked
We spent all our time together
Country dancing or in church
When you left me on that morning
You said I'll see you later Skye

I love you, my caffeine junkie
We kissed; you waved goodbye
How was I to know that was the last time I would see you?
How was I to know how I would feel so lost and lonely too
How was I to know how lonely I would feel without you?
How was I to know that lonely means a void unfulfilled?
How was I to know that lonely means a heart that's killed?
So many thousands of others
Probably feel the same way too
Because on 9/11, how many lost? No one knew
Later we found out the answer
Almost three thousand had died that day
And thousands more were left behind
Grieving and trying to be brave
And although it may sound crazy
I can't think of it; so many feel the same way too
Some lost loved ones, some lost children
We lost so many heroes, some known and many unknown too
Yet I can't even begin to imagine what each one is going through
I only know that loneliness has paved a way for me
To feel depressed and self absorbed in my never-ending grief

My Reflection

By Francine Skye Lentini
11/25/02

When I look into a mirror
I don't recognize what I see
The person staring at me
Just doesn't look like me

I see a hollow person
Without anything inside
Just an empty tired vessel
That always seems to cry

I can't come to terms
With saying a final good-bye
I thought I could at his memorial
I tried, but my heart denied

Why do some say it's normal
To feel like this right now
I'm conflicted and I'm grieving
I try, but don't know how

So I jot down my feelings
I just write what I feel
But the reflection in the mirror
Scares me as my pain's revealed

Every Time

By Francine Skye Lentini
11/25/02

Every time I think I have a friend
It's one less friend I have

Every time I think I'll feel better
Something else makes me feel sad

Every time I think I am forging ahead
I walk backwards in reply

And every time I think I will laugh
Is another time I cry

An Unusual Weekend With You

By Francine Skye Lentini
12/08/02

This has been a strange weekend
Nothing seemed to go right
Yet nothing was really wrong
I guess I was just uptight

Friday was my birthday
But it didn't go as planned
Marisa and Chris both fell ill
Plans postponed, I'd understand

So I took Chris to the doctor
He was given a pill or two
And one was for Marisa
Because she was ill with asthma too

We filled them in the drugstore
And then I took him home to rest
And early on Saturday morning
He had to take two tests

But earlier on my birthday
At some time around noon
Chris said," Mom check the mail please,
I think most of it's for you"

Earlier I thought of the roses
That I did not get this year
I felt sad because no roses
Meant that you really weren't here

So when I went to open the mail
Since most of it was mine
There was a medal, a gift from a mission
That I contribute to sometimes

Another was from the Little Flower Mission
A gift inside had been enclosed
They said it was to renew my membership
Would you believe it was a red rose?

They didn't know it was my birthday
How could it arrive on that day?
They said each member could get only one
Even if you added others to pray

Now it could just be a coincidence
But it seems too hard to ignore
I received it on my birthday
Right after thinking I'd get no more

Somehow you wanted to tell me
That you knew my birthday was here
And you must have asked St. Theresa
To do this favor for me this year

The next day on a Saturday
I was invited to a gathering for me
To celebrate my birthday
With my entire family

Chris and Marisa couldn't come
They were both still ill
And I didn't take my Kari Bear
Theresa's asthma bothered her still

Now I was listening to country music
Christmas music on a CD
And I was remembering all the times
That you would sing those songs with me

I tried to remove my rosary
From the rear view mirror and then
I found it was totally raveled
And I tried and tried again.

I couldn't unravel the rosary
So I listened to the song once more
As I gazed into the rear view mirror
I could not believe what I saw

It looked like a dark cloud was forming
But then an image became refined
And I gasped and cried when I saw it
For it was your face that reflected, not mine

I could see you really clearly
I was shocked, could not say words
But the image I saw so distinctly
Disappeared so I cried unobserved

When I left my sister Theresa
And began the drive back home
I reached again for the rosary beads
And they simply became undone

So I said my prayers in the car now
Thanking God to let me see
Your reflection in my mirror
It had meant the world to me

Now later that same evening
I got a call from my friend Joan
She is superstitious, and very religious
And says she feels what's going on

She said that you're around me
Not liking what you see
You are tired of seeing me depressed
And I'm disturbing the peace you need

Then she told me a strange thing
She said wear red underwear to bed
She said that you might join me there
But only if I wore red

I thought this must be Joan's imagination
This must be a superstitious tale
I went to bed in my normal pajamas
And fell asleep soon without fail

When I awoke the next morning
I was shocked at what was there
On the pillow next to mine in bed
Laid panties; a red pair

I had found them in my drawer
With my other lingerie
I knew they were not my size
So I decided to give them away

I added them to a bag of clothes
That I had prepared for the poor
And I did not see them on my pillow
Just the night before

As I said before this weekend was strange
It made no sense at all
I do believe that you sent me signs
To tell me you recalled

On Sunday I went with Chris and Marisa
To "Lentini's" restaurant to eat
Where we saw the show at Radio City
And to Rockefeller Center; to see the tree

Although the things I wrote tonight
Might appear to be weird
I knew that you were telling me
That you have been right here

You knew I was sad on my birthday
And that I have been missing you so much
You made a plan with St. Theresa
To send a rose; your special touch

And then you asked the Lord to show me
Your face just one more time
And you wanted me to know you lay beside me
In our bed, both yours and mine

So although it seemed a weird birthday
It was most beautiful in it's own way
I knew you showed your loving presence
I pray that it remains with me to stay

Do You?

By Francine Skye Lentini
12/12/02

Do you ever feel like you're losing it
And you don't know where it went?
You walk into a meeting
And then wonder why they met?
You look around, feel out of place
Then ask, "Did I forget?"

Do you find yourself thinking
That you have so many things to do?
Still distracted by daily problems
That are overwhelming you

Do you feel like you lose track of things
You want to do or say?
And when it's over do you ask
"How did so much time slip away?"

Do you ever have a feeling?
Like your mind has gone awry?
And while searching for it's meaning
Life just keeps passing by?

Do you sometimes act intuitively
And then think you've hit the mark?
Then suddenly wake up realizing
You dreamt it in the dark

Do you ever try to conquer
All the problems in one day?
But your energy and motivation
Silently slip from you away

Do you ever wonder "Why can't I tackle things
That I've tackled once before?"
Or do your feelings pile high
Leaving the real reason hidden
So that real reason can be denied

I've Gotta' Tell Jack

By Francine Skye Lentini
12/13/02

How long does it take to convince your mind?
That someone you love has run out of time
Every time I think of something to say
Or of something that I must ask of Blu
I turn around and look for you

Sometimes it's something funny that I heard someone
   say
Sometimes it's a silly thing, that happened during the
   day
Sometimes it's when I see something you would buy
And I would try to convince you that you needed a
   larger size

You've always been a part of me; we could read each
   other's minds
We always talked things over and we always shared our
   time
You were such a part of me; such an extraordinary man
That I felt I could tell you anything and that you would
   understand

When I shop for Christmas presents and I see
   something that you'd like
I stop myself from buying it; I think you're only in my
   mind

When I wrap gifts, and I look for the ribbons and the
   tape
It was you who cut the pieces and tied the ribbon in its
   place

And now when I have a bad dream and I wake up in our
   bed
I look at the empty pillow and the space that you have
   left
So every time I seek your comfort, your advice or your
   gift of tact
The words that keep repeating in my mind are - "I've
   Gotta Tell Jack"

Families Change

By Francine Skye Lentini
12/15/02

Where do I fit in?
That's the question of the day
At least that's what I arrived at
After some thoughtful debate
Do I fit into a family of one?
Or does that mean I am all alone?
I have a wonderful son
Who's grown with a life of his own

I have the most wonderful parents
That there could ever be
But they have each other 55 years
That partnership does not include me
And what about my sisters
One has her husband by her side
The other has a husband and two children
They all know on whom to rely
When they eat their evening's dinner
Their family is sitting right there
They have others right beside them
For their meals and evening prayers

Where do I fit in?
Some of my friends who are single
May relate to what I mean
It's how one defines "family"

That determines how it seems
I think of a family as a group
Who live together and care
They work toward shared goals
And they synchronize their prayers
They are waiting for each other
When they come home at night
To cuddle with or to talk to
To share a purpose in their life

Some families have been altered
Some changed by man's own hand
Others have been changed by fate
God sometimes has other plans
But some who live together
Never seem willing enough to share
Others' thoughts and others' feelings
Others' worries and others' cares

Sometimes families change
Because children who are grown
Move on with their own lives
To start families of their own
So again I ask if I am a family
Where do I fit in?
Since Jack has been taken away from me
My family's worn very thin

How Can I Love Again?

By Francine Skye Lentini
12/18/02

How can I love again?
You were the best of all men
Together we laughed
The best times we passed
If only we could love now as then

How do I live my life?
After being your darlin' wife?
Nothing now lasts
I think of the past
When everything was always all right

I Know It's Going to Happen

By Francine Skye Lentini
1/11/03

I know it's going to happen
It's just a matter of time
That this journal I've been writing
Will be published, that's no lie
I've been writing about my feelings
Since September 11th, 2001
And my emotions going up and down
And how I sometimes wish to run

I know it's going to happen
This book is dedicated to you
And to all those unsung heroes
Whose lives were cut short too
It will be a source for mourners
Emotions released as they read
My poems express deep sadness
The pain, the agony of grief

I know it's going to happen
That thousands who feel like me
Will turn victims into survivors
To quench their emotional need
To allow expression of pent feelings

To be expressed; to be released
To help those who want to heal
To find consolation and to find peace

I know it's going to happen
I've even helped in my own way
I've queried agents and publishers
Explaining what I have to say
I have already been rejected
By more than just a few
But I only need to find one
Who believes and trusts me too

I know it's going to happen
I keep finding things to write
Your inspiration is within me
And for you I'll win this fight
Many people have been saying
That when they read my poems they cry
They can release the pent up sadness
That they keep locked up inside

I know it's going to happen
It's a calling deep in my soul
To honor all the unsung heroes
Your stories need to be told
So others, like me, who read them
Thousands mourning still I'm sure
Can find serenity and comfort
And a possible emotional cure

I know it's going to happen
I left my special reason for last

I have a heart full of emotions
Breaking apart and bleeding fast
And the only way I can heal it
Or at least where I can start
Is for me to write these feelings down
Since they've been tearing me apart

My poetic journal will be a gift
For me, for you, and for many others
The unsung heroes so many have missed
For the brave ones and the fine ones
Who were tragically killed that day
And for all those through their tears
Still trying to find their own way

The Silliest Things

By Francine Skye Lentini
1/24/03

The silliest things remind me of you
Little packs of crackers and cookies too
The spot where you sat on the couch
The bed seems empty and bigger somehow
A cowboy shirt or a pair of boots
A magazine ad could remind me of you

Christmas decorations or magnets on the fridge
A mug with your name; a song by Travis Tritt
A movie we saw over and over again
Always caught the middle-never the end
The Jets Green; the Yankees Blue
Ranger tickets for you, Chris and crew
These types of things remind me of you

The Super Bowl, Pennsylvania and lots of snow
Bouquets of flowers and plants to grow
An empty chair at the table, a setting bare
Books unread on your desk down there
Western clothes and romantic cards
Western charm, a made up yarn
A voice that sings so fine, so true
These are the things that remind me of you

George Strait, Garth Books, Tanya Tucker for sure
Nashville, Printer's Alley, and so much more

Summer sunshine and Promised Land State Park
Our dog, our family, our life, our hearts
Everything around me seems to remind me in part
Of our true love together and our lives torn apart

Tonight's Thoughts

By Francine Skye Lentini
1/31/03

Tonight I spoke to my doctor
And explained the problem I face
Returning to my daily grind
Without your loving face
The last time I went to work
You were home with me
You said "Come here and give me a kiss,
You little caffeine junkie"
I remember your reminding me
That the primary was that night
I never thought I'd relive that day
Every day of my life
Monday I will return to school
My coffee not prepared for me
Your kiss will not wake me up
We will not talk of the day to be
I will warm my car up for myself
If it snows I will clean it too
I will not need to drive you to the subway
I will drive myself to school
Once there I will try to forget
The last day I was there, when I cried
As I saw the Twin Towers tumbling
And knowing you were trapped inside
Monday I'll try to start over
At least with my life's work at school

I'll take it one day at a time now
Until I retire and decide what to do
At some point in the future I will make them
These choices I will then have to face
But right now I'll try to get through Monday
And keep hoping that my heart doesn't break

How Dare You?

By Francine Skye Lentini
3/1/03

How could you just sit there and smile at me
Your face in that frame is all that I see
I can't see you breathing or walking towards me
I don't get to hear you talking to me
How dare you leave me alone this way?
You said you were the one who would positively stay
You were the only one who stood up to me
You taught me how to live and you set me free
Now that you're gone and I'm here all alone
I look at your picture, and I want you home
You said you would love me until eternity
Then you left me here, alone, in misery
You told me to enjoy life every minute that I'm here
That's how you lived yours; it was perfectly clear
How dare you leave and leave me behind
I don't want to start over; it's a waste of my time
It took me forty-five years to find someone like you
Now look at what you've gone and put me through
Was loving you worth all the pain I now feel?
How dare you show me how love feels for real?
I keep looking at the picture of your smiling face
I still want you here; why are you gone from this place?
I love you so much I cry as I say;
"Why did you have to leave me this way?"

You Want A Piece of Me?

By Francine Skye Lentini
3/14/03

You want a piece of me?
What do you want?
Tell me what it is
It's yours

You want a piece of me?
Take it
It ain't doin' me no good
I can't help myself
I fall apart
Who gives a shit?

You want a piece of me?
Maybe you want my ears
Know what they hear?
Stop being weak!
You could do better than this!
It's your own fault anyway!
You should have done it right the first time
Therapists saying
Think of yourself before anyone else
Make sense of it
Learn to say no

Your brain's breaking down
Get it together girl!

You want a piece of me?
Tell me what it is
This screwed up mind
It's shot
Can't think anymore
Muddled
Befuddled
Betwixed and Between
Go up or down?
Think it through
Think what?

You want a piece of me?
Do you want this soul?
It's sore
But that's not a body part
That's spiritual, right?
Still it's a piece of me
Isn't it?
It's been through war

You want a piece of me?
You want this tongue
It just wants to scream
To curse
To yell at anyone
Don't you get it yet?
This is not me!
Who are you looking for anyway?
I yell at me too

You want a piece of me?
What do you want?
My eyes
You could have them
They're no use to me
I don't see happiness
Consolation
Peace
I see shit

You want a piece of me?
How 'bout my nose?
It smells shit
You won't like how it smells
Shit piled high
Getting higher
And you know how shit is
Slippery
Stinky
Undesirous to the nose
You can never rise to the top of it
You can just fall into it

You want a piece of me?
What do you want?
This brain
My intelligence
What's that?
It's all a game
People play you
They use and abuse you
They give you love

Ha! Wait and see what happens then!
They die
You die
Your emotions die
But the jokes on you
You're still here
So what now?

You want a piece of me?
Make it perfectly clear
Which piece do you want?
It's not for sale
I'll give it to you
You figure it out
You'll get as crazy as me
No doubt

You want a piece of me?
So which piece do you want?
Each is a disaster
You have answers
Yeah right
Why should I care?
For what?
Go figure

The Book Comes Together

By Francine Skye Lentini
4/2/03

I don't think I'm a poet
But I started writing poems
My artist wanted to do the cover
She had ideas of her own
The "editor" asked, "Me edit?"
"Is that what you want me to do?"
"I'm not an editor, just a teacher
Who happens to believe in you"

What a peculiar group we are
Thrown together simply by choice
All working from different directions
With a common thread of voice
I wanted this book to be published
But I had no idea how to start
Now Cynthia is editing
Ann Marie is painting
And I'm trying to do my part

Although I knew it would happen
That this book I wrote for you
And for all the unsung heroes
Whose honor is long overdue

I just didn't know how to do it
I was too close to edit my own
I have no artistic talent
I needed a publisher to give it its form

But I want it to be perfect
I'll take all the time I need
With a poet, an editor and an artist
My book will become complete
It will show the journey
Of one grieving widow's heart
And of how it once was happy
And how now it's ripped apart

And if the book helps others
With a broken heart to heal
Then it will soothe my heart and soul
And satisfy a need that's real

Do You Hear Me?

By Francine Skye Lentini
7/3/03

Do you hear me?
What's wrong with you?
You look so fine
You're not feeling better?
I think it's about time
Just let it go
Your pain still shows
You know the truth
I'm not hiding from you
Those people you see
Are not really me
They're your imagination gone wild
You're not a child
You know I was found
And buried in the ground
Almost two years has passed
Get off your ass
get "out there"
Find friends who care
Meet new people
Grow
You have more living to do

So
Move on with your life
Take love as it comes

Cherish it while it lasts
Sometimes love passes
Just look at me
Never made 53
Cut off with many unfinished plans
But not the plan of God's own hand

You're luckier than most
You have belief and prayers
Don't ever believe
They fall on deaf ears

So
My dearest wife
I can't be in your life
But I can be a part
Of your large loving heart
And
You can take me wherever you go
And you can take me with you
As you begin life anew
Mourn no more for me
You've work to do
To fulfill your own destiny
So
My beautiful heart
My cowgirl Skye
Start living again
Before you too, die